evidence in

Diabetes

and Cardiovascular Disease

by Eugene Hughes

MERCK SHARP & DOHME

Provided as a service to medicine
by Merck Sharp & Dohme Ltd

Evidence in Diabetes and Cardiovascular Disease
Eugene Hughes

Published in the UK by:
National Services for Health Improvement
The Horseshoes, Church Road
Cressing, Essex CM77 8PQ

Copyright 2009 National Services for Health Improvement

Printed in the UK by Stephens and George Ltd.

ISBN 978-0-9560921-0-6

About the Author

Irish-born in 1956, Eugene qualified from Guy's Hospital in 1979. He works as a general practitioner in Ryde on the Isle of Wight.

In 1996, he was a founder member of Primary Care Diabetes UK. He served on the committee for six years, during which time he was involved in conference organisation.

More recently, he was a member of the steering group which established the Primary Care Diabetes Society in the UK.

In 2002 he joined the executive of Primary Care Diabetes Europe, and has organised several international conferences. He is currently chairman of this organisation. In 2007, the journal *Primary Care Diabetes* was launched, and has recently gained *Medline* listing.

He was the editor of the *Diabetes and Primary Care* journal from 1998 - 2007. He is also on the editorial board of *Diabetes Digest* and the *European Endocrine Review*.

He has written many articles and editorials on diabetes, particularly relating to service delivery and early management of type 2 diabetes. He is the medical editor of *A Simple Guide to Diabetes*.

Contents

Introduction

Diabetes is a serious progressive disease. Sufferers are exposed to an elevated risk of cardiovascular disease, and may die prematurely.

Effective management of the condition demands that we focus not only on the management of hyperglycaemia, but also of hypertension and dyslipidaemia.

In order to do this, we are encouraged to practice 'evidence-based' medicine. But what is the evidence? Is it easy to assimilate, accessible and unassailably robust?

How confident are we that our treatment and management decisions are based on sound and incontrovertible research findings? We may be called upon to defend our actions to our peers, to prescribing advisors, or even to a court of law. Factors such as cost of new therapies and medical jurisprudence may influence what we do in practice.

When approaching the evidence, there is a tendency to be confused by the jargon surrounding statistical analysis and study design. What exactly is a 'p' value? What is an 'intention to treat analysis'?

Over the years, I have had to rely on the generosity and patience of more academically-minded friends and colleagues to interpret some of the finer points of new studies, as well as lessons learned from established studies, which may have a direct impact on my management of people with diabetes in the practice setting.

At a time when we are presented with a plethora of new treatments, and ever-tighter prescribing regulations, I felt it was important to have a handy reference guide which would not only summarise the main findings from several relevant studies, but also provide an overview of medical statistics, and some insights into research methodology.

For each study, I have devised a simple format, which will hopefully make interpretation simple:

WHO

- ◆ Who were the authors of the study ?
- ◆ Who were the study population ?

WHERE

- ◆ Where was the study undertaken?

WHEN

- ◆ When were the results published?

WHY

- ◆ What was the purpose of the trial or study?

WHAT

- ◆ What were the results?
- ◆ What are the lessons we can learn?

I hope you will find this simple guide interesting, perhaps invaluable, and that it will make a small contribution to your care of people with diabetes.

Chapter One:

a

b

$P=0.001$

An Introduction to Statistics

▮▮ An Introduction to Statistics

Mean

Also known as the average; the sum of all the values, divided by the number of values.

Example:
Four people attend the clinic; their weights are 98kg, 100kg, 102kg, and 104kg. The mean weight is 98 + 100 + 102 + 104 = 404, divided by 4 = 101kg.

Median

This is the point at which half the values are above, and half the values are below.

Example:
In the example above, the median value is also 101kg, as half the values are above this point, and half below.

Mode

The commonest value in a set of results.

Example:
As the clinic progresses, the recorded weights are (in kg) 98, 100, 100, 100, 102, 104, and 105. The mode is 100kg.

Bi-modal distribution

Occurs when the values are placed on a graph, and there are two 'peaks'.

A bi-modal distribution may mean that there are two separate sorts of group in the sample, so that an average value is not a suitable measure.

Standard deviation

Standard deviation only applies to data that are normally distributed. A standard deviation indicates how much a set of values is spread around the average.

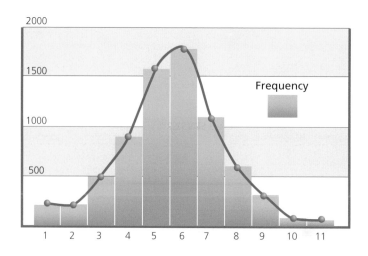

◆ One standard deviation above and below the mean will include 68.2% of all values. This is abbreviated to **± 1 SD**.

◆ Two standard deviations above and below the mean (**± 2 SD**) will include 95.4% of all values.

◆ Three standard deviations above and below the mean (**± 3 SD**) will include 99.7% of all values.

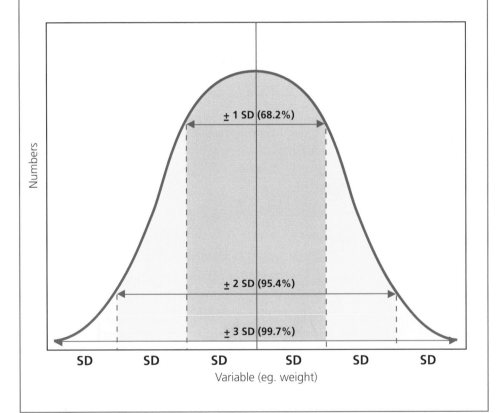

Figure 1: Standard deviation

Confidence interval

When we undertake a study, it is impossible to use the whole population, so a sample is used. Clearly, we hope that the sample will be representative of the population we wish to study, and that the results obtained from the study, using a sample, will be applicable to the whole population.

However, we know from experience that we may get a different result by using a different sample.

Supposing we want to test the effectiveness of a new weight reducing drug? Sample A given the drug for a year had a mean weight loss of 3kg. Sample B given the drug for a year had a mean weight loss of 4kg.

Ideally, we want to know what the mean weight loss would be if the whole population was given the drug for a year – the 'true value'.

The confidence interval shows the range in which we can be confident that this 'true value' lies, and this can be calculated statistically. It is usual to use 95% confidence intervals (95% CI). In the above example, we might say that the 95% CI is 2kg-5kg, ie we are 95% sure that even though sample A had a mean weight loss of 3kg, the 'true value' (of the whole population) would be between 2kg and 5kg. If our 95% CI included the value of 0, it would mean that there was a 5% chance that there was no weight loss with the drug.

The size of the CI is related to the sample size. Larger studies usually mean a narrower CI.

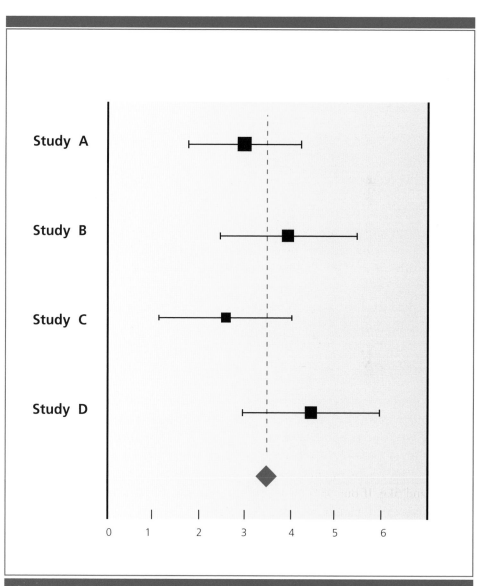

Figure 2: Forest plot

If we plot the mean weight loss with 95% CI from several studies with different sample sizes, we can see an overall estimate of effect.

This is called a Forest plot. The combined estimate has a smaller CI, giving a more accurate estimate of the treatment effect.

'P' values

When a trial is undertaken, we may expect to see a difference between the groups. However, we usually start with the hypothesis that there is **no difference** between the treatments. This is known as the **null hypothesis** – that any difference is due to chance, not the treatment. So we theoretically set out to say 'if we put group A on one drug and group B on another drug, there will be no difference in outcomes. If that turns out to be the result, the null hypothesis has been proved (increasingly unlikely in modern pharmaceutical research). If a difference between the groups is detected, we then say, 'Ah, but that probably happened by chance. If we repeated the trial several times, at least one of the sets of results would show no difference.' By adopting this seemingly negative stance, we challenge ourselves to be able to say 'Well actually, the difference between the groups was so great, that you would have to do the study a thousand times over before one set of results proved the null hypothesis – in other words, the chances of that happening are amazingly small.' The 'p' or 'probability' value is just that – the probability that any difference between the groups would have happened by chance.

If $p = 0.5$, then the probability that the difference happened by chance is 50% or 50:50 – not very convincing.

If $p = 0.05$, that probability becomes 5%, or 1 in 20. Clearly the smaller the p value, the more unlikely it is that the observed difference happened by chance – it happened because of the treatment effect.

I am sorry to labour this point, but a good understanding of p values is essential to interpret trial results. Different levels of p value equate to different levels of statistical significance:

$p = 0.01$ is referred to as highly significant;
            a **1 in 100** probability that the difference
            happened by chance

$p = 0.001$ is referred to as very highly significant;
            a **1 in 1,000** probability that the difference
            happened by chance

Odds ratio

A concept which is used to look at factors which might have a negative effect on the study population. Suppose we are comparing a new treatment for arthritis with placebo, and are concerned about the risk of gastrointestinal bleeding.

An odds ratio of 1 indicates no difference in risk between the groups, so the odds of having a GI bleed are the same in both groups.

An odds ratio of >1 indicates that the number of events of GI bleeding is greater in the treated group.

An odds ratio of <1 indicates that the number of events of GI bleeding is less in the treated group.

An odds ratio of 1.5 means that you are 50% more likely to suffer a GI bleed in the treatment group.

Odds ratios are often quoted with 95% confidence intervals. If the confidence interval does not contain the value 1.0, then it is statistically significant *(see below)*.

Risk reduction

Pharmaceutical companies often produce detail aids which trumpet '50% relative risk reduction!' This is all very well, but in order to understand how important it is, we need to know the absolute risk (AR). For example, if the risk of death from cancer of the lung in a population of non-smokers is 1 in 1,000, but five years' treatment with drug A reduced it to 1 in 2,000, then the relative risk reduction is 50%, but the absolute risk reduction is small, and 1,000 people would have to be treated for five years to bring about a small benefit.

The absolute risk reduction is the improvement in the intervention group – the improvement in the control group = 0.05%. Another way of looking at this is numbers needed to treat (NNT). This is calculated by NNT = 100/AR, in this case 100/0.05 = 2,000. NNT is often used in economic arguments; the lower the NNT, the more cost-effective the treatment is deemed to be. You will also come across the term number needed to harm (NNH), which inverts the concept to look at how many subjects need to be treated to suffer an adverse event.

Life tables and Kaplan-Meier plots

Life tables look at survival data at a number of fixed time points and calculate the survival rate at those points. The most commonly used method is the Kaplan–Meier plot. The resulting plots are able to compare survival between groups *(see example)*.

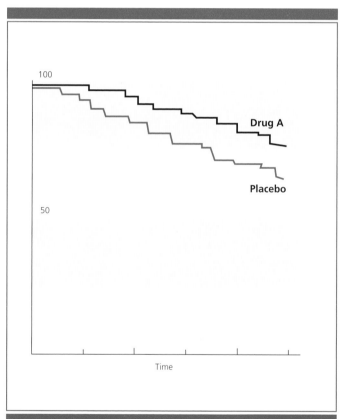

Figure 3: Kaplan-Meier plot

Sensitivity and specificity

These terms are often used for screening for a disease or condition. Unless the test is perfect, there will be times when the test is positive, but the person does not have the disease – this is called a 'false positive'. There will also be times when the test will be negative, but the patient does in fact have the disease. This is a 'false negative'.

Sensitivity shows how often the test will be positive if the disease is present - the 'pick-up' rate.

Specificity shows how often the test will be negative if the disease is absent – the 'exclude-it' rate.

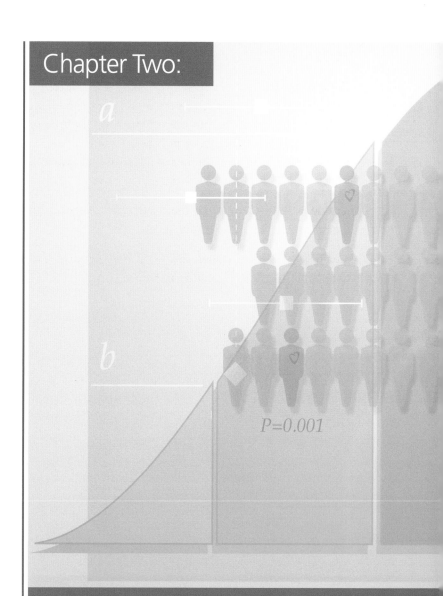

Chapter Two:

a

b

$P=0.001$

Clinical Trials

██ Clinical Trials

In order to evaluate the effectiveness of new forms of treatment, a clinical trial is performed. This may be undertaken to assess new or existing drug therapy, surgical procedures, diets, educational intervention, or alternative therapies.

Taking clinical trials on drugs as the example, there are four categories:

Phase I	Clinical pharmacology and toxicology
Phase II	Initial clinical investigation
Phase III	Full scale evaluation of treatment
Phase IV	Post-marketing surveillance

The process of developing a drug from its formulation in the laboratory through to its eventual marketing is a very long, laborious and expensive affair, which is closely regulated.

Controlled clinical trials commonly compare a new drug treatment with existing therapies or placebo. To be effective, the trail should compare two groups of people who differ only with respect to their treatment. The 'gold standard' for trial design is considered to be the **randomised, double-blind controlled trial**.

Randomisation

If the two groups to be compared differ in some way, there is the possibility of **bias**. This may be in the form of **volunteer bias**, for example when people who present for a study are perhaps younger and healthier than the intended treatment group, or **selection bias**, when the people running the trial choose a group of people who are more likely to attend and complete the study, possibly more intelligent or more mobile. To avoid bias, **randomisation** is important. This can take many forms, the simplest being alternate allocation to one group, then the other. Stratified randomisation is sometimes used to reduce inequalities in groups.

In **parallel** group design, both groups are studied concurrently. In **crossover** group design, both groups of patients are given both treatments in sequence. This can be problematic, however, as some patients may drop out after one treatment, and so fail to complete the study, and there may be a 'carry-over' effect from one period to the next, so that the results obtained from the second period are affected by the treatment in the first period.

In a **factorial design**, two treatments are simultaneously compared with each other and a control, there are thus four groups; A, B, A+B, and placebo *(see fig 4)*.

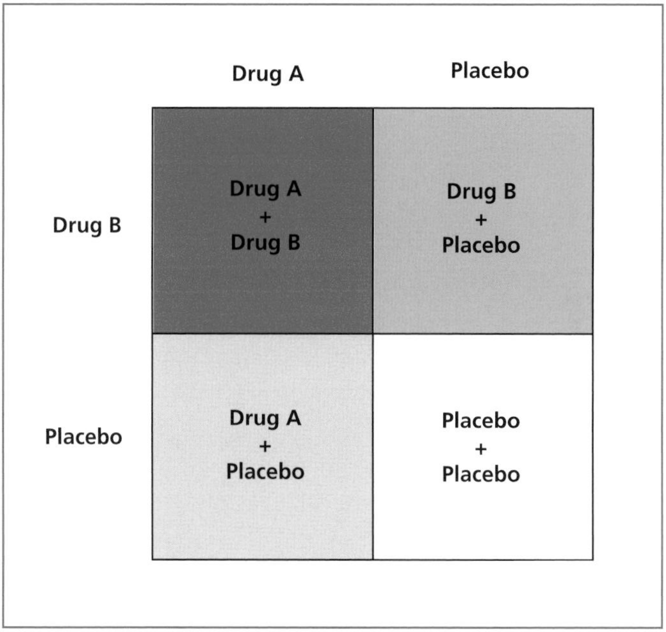

Figure 4: Factorial design

Double-blind trials

In most cases, it is desirable that neither the patient nor the trial manager knows which treatment is given. In **double-blind trials**, this involves the use of dummy tablets or capsules which are identical to the active treatment. In **single-blind** trials, only the patient is unaware which treatment is being taken.

Placebo effect

Many drug trials compare an active drug to placebo – the 'dummy drug' in blinded trials. This is because the simple act of taking a tablet in itself can bring benefits to some patients. On the other hand, patients taking a placebo will often experience side-effects, such as headache or lethargy. This is the **placebo effect**, so it is important to know how the active drug **differs** from placebo. In trials of drugs used to lower blood sugar, for example, it is important to know what happens to blood sugar levels in the placebo group over time, as this may improve any benefit shown by the active drug. As diabetes is a progressive disorder, blood sugar levels may deteriorate over time. If, in a study, the placebo group show a 0.2% **deterioration** in HbA1c, whilst the treated group show a 0.6% **improvement** in HbA1c, then the actual (or placebo-subtracted) benefit is 0.8%.

Inclusions and exclusions

It is a criticism often levelled at drug trial populations that they do not represent a real population, and therefore inferences from trial data are not necessarily applicable to a normal population. This is because there are usually **inclusion and exclusion criteria** which place restrictions on those eligible to take part. For example, some clinical trials exclude people over 75, those with dementia, those with a diagnosis of malignancy, or those previously treated with similar drugs. Can the results of such trials truly be applicable to the motley assortment of individuals who present to us in primary care?

Outcomes

Trials should specify a **primary endpoint**, namely the main point on which the trial data will be analysed. Sometimes, **secondary endpoints** are specified pre-trial, and providing they are rigorously monitored, can provide useful information (see the ProActive study). It is also possible to conduct a **sub-group analysis**, for example, if a drug designed to reduce myocardial infarction failed to meet its primary endpoint, subsequent analysis of certain groups – women, over-60s – may show statistically significant benefits. **Post-hoc analysis** looks at what happens to a group after the trial has finished. Does the 'treatment effect' persist, or does the 'active' group fare the same as the 'placebo' group after, say, 10 years?

Power

The **power** of a trial is the probability that the study can detect a real difference, which will be statistically significant. For example, you might want to show that antibiotic A is better than placebo B in treating chest infections. If you treat 50 people with A, and give 50 people B, then discover that 48 people in group A got better, whereas only three people in group B got better, it is likely that the drug works, so a small sample size would be acceptable. However, if you want to show that new drug X is better than old drug Y at preventing cardiovascular disease, you will have to show that the number of people developing cardiovascular disease over a given period of time (years) is significantly different. Suppose 45 people in group X suffer myocardial infarction as opposed to 50 people in group Y; the study has to be **powered** to show that the difference did not happen by chance. This may mean recruiting thousands of people in each group. There are complicated formulae and tables to calculate sample size in relation to power.

Protocol violations

In many trials, patients will have failed to follow the trial protocol – they may have stopped taking the medication, may take 'disallowed' therapies, or may even have been ineligible from the start. The only practical way to deal with this is to keep all randomised patients in the trial for the purpose of analysis. This is known as **'intention to treat'** analysis, as it was indeed your intention to treat all patients according to the trial protocol. Clearly, the effect this will have on the outcome will depend on the number and type of protocol violations. It may seem strange, but the alternative is to exclude randomised patients based on subjective decisions, which might introduce bias.

A **completer analysis**, however, only uses data from those participants who remained in the study.

Meta-analysis

Over a period of time there may be several clinical trials using the same drug, with possibly different outcome measures. It may be possible to perform an overview or **meta-analysis**, by means of a structured statistical analysis from several published (or unpublished, in certain circumstances) trials. A picture might emerge from this sort of analysis which may indicate wider generalisability of results than is warranted by a single trial. Rarer adverse events may also achieve a greater significance. In recent years, several prominent figures have published meta-analyses which have sparked fierce debate, particularly in the thiazolidinedione arena.

Cohort study

This refers to a non-experimental study that follows a group of people (a cohort), with the intention of analysing how events differ among people within the group. This can be useful to determine whether exposure to a suspected risk factor, eg alcohol or industrial chemicals, leads to differences in outcomes within the group. Prospective cohort studies which track participants forward in time are more reliable than retrospective cohort studies.

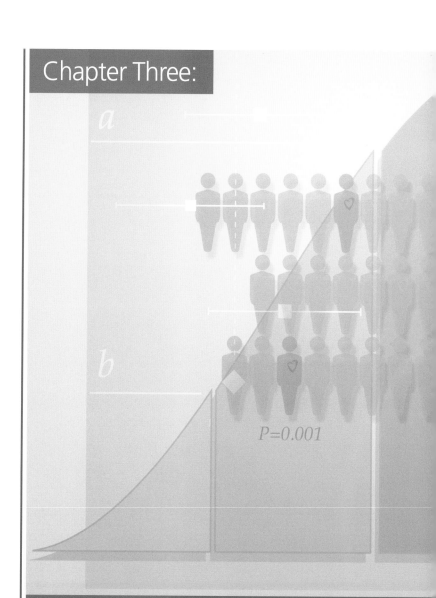

Chapter Three:

P=0.001

Levels of Evidence

■■ Levels of Evidence

With so much evidence accumulating from thousands of clinical trials, how can we hope to make sense of it all?

There are some established hierarchical structures for grading of evidence. An example is given below:

Grade 1   Well conducted, suitably powered randomised controlled trials

Grade 2   Well conducted, but small and underpowered randomised controlled trials

Grade 3   Systematic reviews and meta-analyses

Grade 4   Non-randomised observational studies

Grade 5   Non-randomised studies with historical control

Grade 6   Case series without control

Exact methods vary, but higher precedence is always given to randomised controlled trials and systematic reviews.

The Cochrane Library

The Cochrane library is a collection of databases in medicine and other healthcare specialities founded by the Cochrane collaboration. At its core is a database of systematic reviews and meta-analyses which summarise and interpret the results of high quality medical research. The Cochrane library aims to make the results of well-controlled trials readily available. It is a key resource in evidence-based medicine.

The National Library for Health (NLH)

This offers easy and quick access to high quality knowledge, information and services for healthcare professionals, managers and patients.

www.library.nhs.uk

Clinical Evidence (BMJ publishing) is a key part of the NLH. It can be used by clinicians:

◆ To find information on specific patient cases

◆ To help inform conversation with colleagues

◆ To develop protocols and guidelines

◆ To discuss treatment options with patients

◆ For training and learning

◆ For preparing presentations and papers

Clinical Evidence uses the following categorisation of treatment effects:

Beneficial

Interventions whose effectiveness has been demonstrated by clear evidence from randomised controlled trials, and expectation of harm that is small compared with the benefits.

Likely to be beneficial

Interventions for whom effectiveness is less well established than for those listed under 'beneficial'.

Trade off between benefit and harms

Interventions for which clinicians and patients should weigh up the beneficial and harmful effects according to the individual circumstances and priorities.

Unknown effectiveness

Interventions for which there are currently insufficient data or data of inadequate quality.

Unlikely to be beneficial

Interventions for which lack of effectiveness is less well established than for those listed under 'likely to be ineffective or harmful'.

Likely to be ineffective or harmful

Interventions whose effectiveness or harmfulness has been demonstrated by clear evidence.

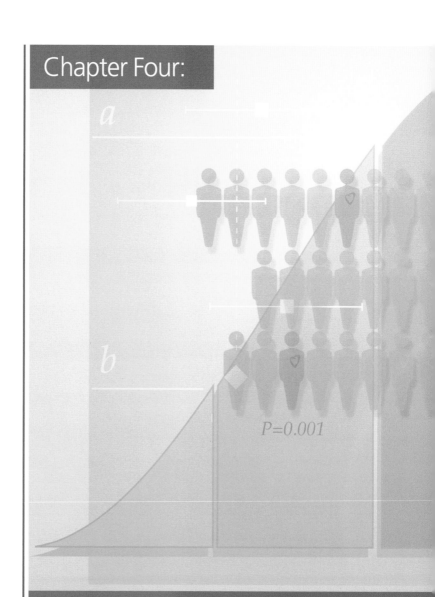

Chapter Four:

a

b

$P=0.001$

The Studies

4S

The Scandinavian simvastatin survival study

WHO

4,444 patients with angina pectoris or previous myocardial infarction, with cholesterol levels of 5.5 to 8.0 mmol/L

WHERE

Multicentre study in Scandinavia

Published in the *Lancet* 344:1383-89

WHEN

1994

WHY

To determine the effect of cholesterol lowering with simvastatin on mortality and morbidity in patients with coronary heart disease

Randomised to placebo (2,223) or simvastatin (2,221)

Primary endpoint was total mortality

Median follow-up of 5.4 years

WHAT

Compared to placebo, the simvastatin group had a relative risk reduction in death of 30%

There was a 42% reduction in coronary death in the simvastatin group

There was a 37% reduction in the risk of undergoing myocardial revascularisation procedures

Total cholesterol levels decreased by 25% in the simvastatin group, with a 35% reduction in LDL

LEARNING POINT

Long-term treatment with simvastatin is safe and improves survival in coronary heart disease patients

ACCORD

Action to control cardiovascular risk in diabetes

WHO

The ACCORD study group
Sponsored by the National Heart, Lung, and Blood Institute

10,251 patients with type 2 diabetes, with established CVD disease or two risk factors for CVD. Participants had a mean age of 62 and a median HbA1c of 8.1% at study entry. Median duration of diabetes – 10 years

WHERE

77 centres in the USA and Canada

Published in *NEJM* 358: 2545-2559

WHEN

Started 2001 and 2003

WHY

To investigate the advantages or otherwise of tight blood pressure and glycaemic control in a range lower than that currently recommended. Participants were randomised to receive intensive (target HbA1c <6.0%) or standard (target HbA1c 7.0-7.9%) treatment. Primary endpoint was a composite of non-fatal MI, non-fatal stroke, and death from CV causes

WHAT

The intensive blood glucose-lowering arm was discontinued after 3.5 years of follow-up, due to a significant excess of all-cause mortality among intensively treated patients. The median HbA1c in the intensive group was 6.4%; in the standard group it was 7.5%

◆ 257 patients in the intensive therapy group died

◆ 203 patients in the standard therapy group died

Hypoglycaemia episodes requiring assistance, and weight gain of more than 10kg were more common in the intensively treated group

LEARNING POINT

Compared with standard therapy, the use of intensive therapy increased mortality, and did not significantly reduce major CV events. These findings identify a previously unidentified harm of intensive glucose lowering in high risk patients with type 2 diabetes. Analyses performed to date have not identified any clear explanation for the higher mortality (compared with ADVANCE – see below). There are also blood pressure and lipid lowering arms of the study (not yet reported)

ADOPT

A diabetes outcome progression trial

WHO

Kahn, SE, Haffner SM, Hese MA et al
4,360 patients who had not received any previous pharmaco-
logical treatment for newly diagnosed type 2 diabetes

WHERE

Multicentre study

Published in *NEJM* 355: 2427-43

WHEN

2006

WHY

A double-blind randomised controlled trial to evaluate the
durability of glycaemic control in patients receiving
monotherapy with an insulin sensitizer (rosiglitazone), a
biguanide (metformin), or a sulphonylurea (glibenclamide)

Patients received:

Rosiglitazone	1,456
Metformin	1,454
Glibenclamide	1,441

for a median of four years

Primary endpoint was time to monotherapy failure defined as
fasting glucose of >10.0 mmol/l

WHAT

Monotherapy failed on: 143 patients on rosiglitazone

207 patients on metformin

311 patients on glibenclamide

The cumulative incidence of monotherapy failure at five years was 15% for rosiglitazone, 21% for metformin and 34% for glibenclamide, representing statistically significant risk reductions for rosiglitazone of 32% versus metformin and 63% versus glibenclamide

Over the five years, mean weight increased by 4.8kg in the rosiglitazone group, by 2.9kg in the metformin group, and by 2.2kg in the glibenclamide group

An increased rate of fractures was seen in women in the rosiglitazone group, particularly of small bones of the hands and feet.

LEARNING POINT

Rosiglitazone gave sustained glycaemic control, but with weight gain and an increased risk of fractures in women.

ADVANCE

Action in diabetes and vascular disease: preterax and diamicron MR controlled evaluation

WHO

The Advance Collaborative Group
11,000 people with type 2 diabetes, randomised to intensive or routine blood glucose lowering, and intensive or routine blood pressure lowering. A multicentre, factorial, randomised controlled trial. Participants had an average age of 66 years, with a mean diabetes duration of 8 years. The mean HbA1c at randomisation was 7.5%

WHERE

215 centres in 20 countries including Canada, UK, and Australia

Published in *NEJM* 358; 2560-72

WHEN

2008

WHY

To compare intensive blood pressure lowering and intensive blood glucose lowering with 'routine' treatment. The intensive blood glucose lowering arm involved the use of gliclazide modified release 30-120 mg daily, otherwise glucose lowering therapy was at the clinician's discretion. The primary end points were composites of major microvascular and macrovascular events, assessed both together and separately

WHAT

There was a 0.7% difference between the intensive and routine blood glucose lowering arms at study completion

In the intensive group, there was:

◆ A 21% reduction in nephropathy

◆ A 14% reduction in microvascular events

◆ No significant reduction in macrovascular events

◆ No significant effects on all-cause or cardiovascular mortality

LEARNING POINT

This study shows that intensive blood glucose lowering led to a reduction in microvascular events, particularly renal events, but did not lead to a reduction in macrovascular events (compare ACCORD, above).

Bear in mind that participants had an 8-year duration of diabetes – perhaps earlier intensive control, with avoidance of hypoglycaemia, should be our aim

ALLHAT

The antihypertensive and lipid-lowering treatment to prevent heart attack trial

WHO

A total of 42,418 patients enrolled between 1994 and 1998. The trial continued to 2002. Patients were aged 55 or older with Stage 1 or Stage 2 hypertension and at least one other CVD risk factor. A large percentage of participants were African-American

WHERE

The trial was sponsored by the National Heart, Lung and Blood Institute (NHLBI) in the USA and was conducted in about 600 clinics in the USA, Puerto Rico, the Virgin Islands, and Canada

WHEN

Published in *JAMA* 2002 288: 2981-2997

WHY

The study had two components:

An antihypertensive component, to determine whether newer antihypertensive agents, such as ACE inhibitors, calcium channel blockers, and alpha blockers, reduce the incidence of CHD in high risk hypertensives when compared to diuretics

A lipid lowering component, to determine whether reduction of serum cholesterol with pravastatin reduces total mortality in moderately hypercholesterolaemic older patients

WHAT

ALLHAT demonstrated that a diuretic (chlorthalidone) was superior at preventing CVD events compared to each of the other dugs studied – a calcium channel blocker (amlodipine), an ACE inhibitor (lisinopril) and an alpha-adrenergic blocker (doxazosin). Each of the newer drugs had higher rates of one or more forms of CVD. None of the three test treatments differed significantly from chlorthalidone in rates of major CHD events and all-cause mortality

The doxazosin arm was stopped early (2000) due to a 25% higher rate of combined CVD and a two-fold higher rate of heart failure compared to the diuretic arm

Cholesterol levels fell substantially in the usual care as well as the pravastatin treatment groups. Although the statin group had greater reductions in total cholesterol levels than the usual care group, the difference between the two groups was relatively modest, largely due to increased use of statins in the usual care group

LEARNING POINT

This study showed that thiazide-type diuretics should be drugs of choice for initial treatment of hypertension in most patients requiring drug therapy

Alpha-blockers should not be considered for initial therapy

ASCOT

The Anglo-Scandinavian cardiac outcomes trial

WHO

Dahlof B, Sever PS, Poulter NR, Wedel H et al
19,257 patients with hypertension and at least three pre-specified cardiovascular risk factors such as being over 55 years old, a smoker, and having a family history of coronary events

WHERE

Multicentre study in the UK, Ireland, Sweden, Norway, Denmark, Finland, and Iceland

Published in the *Lancet* 366: 895-906

WHEN

2005

WHY

To compare the regimen of a beta-blocker (atenolol) plus a diuretic (bendroflumethiazide) to the regimen of an ACE inhibitor (perindopril) and a calcium-channel blocker (amlodipine) in the management of hypertension

A separate cholesterol lowering arm looked at whether the addition of a statin (atorvastatin) reduced the number of cardiovascular events and stroke in individuals with hypertension and normal cholesterol levels

WHAT

In November 2004, the ASCOT steering committee endorsed the recommendation of the Data and Safety Monitoring Board to stop the trial early due to the benefits, including mortality demonstrated in patients who received the calcium-channel blocker based regime

The cholesterol lowering arm was stopped after two years because the results showed clear benefits from taking a statin

Patients on the amlodipine based regimen experienced an 11% reduction in total mortality, a 23% reduction in fatal and non-fatal strokes and a 24% reduction in cardiovascular death, compared to patients on the beta-blocker based regimen. In addition, they had a 10% reduction in the primary endpoint of fatal coronary heart disease and non-fatal heart attack, which did not reach statistical significance as the study was halted early due to the mortality benefit associated with the amlodipine based regimen. The study also showed that patients who received the beta-blocker based regimen were at increased risk of new onset diabetes irrespective of all other risk factors, eg increased weight, blood glucose at study entry and initial blood pressure level

LEARNING POINT

Overall, ASCOT concludes that by taking a combination of a calcium-channel blocker and an ACE inhibitor, as well as a statin (regardless of cholesterol level), people with high blood pressure can reduce their risk of heart attack and stroke by more than half

45

CARDS

The collaborative atorvastatin diabetes study

WHO

Colhoun HM, Betteridge DJ, Durrington PN et al
2,838 patients with type 2 diabetes and no documented evidence of cardiovascular disease. They had LDL-cholesterol <4.14 mmol/l, triglycerides <6.78 mmol/l and one of the following: retinopathy, albuminuria, smoker, or hypertension

WHERE

Multicentre study

Published in the *Lancet* 364: 685-96

WHEN

2004

WHY

To assess the effectiveness of atorvastatin 10mg daily for primary prevention of major cardiovascular events in patients with type 2 diabetes without high LDL levels

Primary endpoint was time to first occurrence of acute coronary heart disease event, coronary revascularisation or stroke

WHAT

The trial was terminated two years earlier than expected because the pre-specified early stopping rule for efficacy had been met. Median duration of follow-up was 3.9 years

Treatment with atorvastatin was associated with a 37% reduction in the incidence of major cardiovascular events

Coronary heart disease events were reduced by 36% in the atorvastatin group, stroke by 48%

Atorvastatin reduced the death rate by 27%

LEARNING POINT

This study showed that atorvastatin treatment can prevent cardiovascular disease in patients with type 2 diabetes, even if they do not have high cholesterol levels

Some would say that it ended the debate as to whether ALL patients with type 2 diabetes should be on a statin

DCCT and EDIC
Diabetes control and complications trial and Epidemiology of diabetes interventions and complications

WHO

The Epidemiology of Diabetes Interventions and Complications Research Group

1,441 patients with type 1 diabetes

WHERE

A multicentre trial conducted in the USA and Canada

Published in *NEJM* 342: 381-9

WHEN

DCCT study conducted between 1983 and 1993

WHY

To assess the effects of intensive or conventional insulin treatment on the complications of diabetes

Patients were randomised to conventional insulin treatment (1-2 injections/day), or intensive (3-4 injections/day). The intensive group had a diet and exercise plan, and monthly visits to a healthcare team composed of a physician, nurse educator, dietician, and behavioural therapist

WHAT

At the end of the study, patients in the intensive group had a median HbA1c of 7.3% compared with an HbA1c of 9.1% in the conventional treatment group

The intensive group had 76% reduced risk of retinopathy, 50% reduced risk of nephropathy, and 60% reduced risk of neuropathy

There was an increase in risk of hypoglycaemia in the intensive group, and increased weight gain

What happened next?

Most DCCT patients (95%) were subsequently enrolled in the Epidemiology of Diabetes Interventions and Complications trial (EDIC), an observational study to determine the long-term effects of the intensive or conventional treatment on microvascular complications. The benefits of 6.5 years of intensive therapy on microvascular complications persist for at least a further seven years after the period of intensive implementation, despite worsening of glycaemic control

At the end of EDIC year 1, mean HbA1c levels were 7.9% in the former intensive group, and 8.3% in the former conventional group; the levels then converged further and remained similar during the ensuing seven years

The reduction in risk of retinopathy seen in the DCCT was the same or greater after four years of EDIC; the benefits of intensive therapy did not wane

After six years of EDIC, the risk of new microalbuminuria was 67% lower in the former intensive treatment group compared with the former conventional treatment group. The presence of hypertension at this time was also greater in the former conventional group than in the former intensive group (33% v 25%)

LEARNING POINT

The DCCT/EDIC studies show that early intensive treatment to achieve and maintain tight glycaemic control results in long-term benefits that continue even if control worsens after the initial intensive treatment period. This carry-over effect has been called 'metabolic memory'

DPP

The diabetes prevention programme

WHO

Knowler WC, Barrett-Connor E, Fowler SE et al
Undertaken by the Diabetes Prevention Program Research
Group, USA

WHERE

A multicentre randomised trial in the USA

Published in *NEJM* 2002 346: 393-403

WHEN

2002

WHY

To examine the effect of lifestyle modification or metformin
on the progression to type 2 diabetes in a group of 3,234
non-diabetic people with impaired fasting glucose

Mean age of participants was 51 years, and mean body mass
index was 34

Randomly assigned to placebo treatment, metformin treatment (850mg b.d.), or a lifestyle modification programme with
the goals of at least a 7% weight loss and at least 150 minutes
of physical activity per week

WHAT

Average follow-up was 2.8 years. The incidence of diabetes was 11 cases per 100 person-years in the placebo group. It was 7.8 cases per 100 person-years in the metformin group, and 4.8 cases per 100 person-years in the lifestyle group. The lifestyle intervention reduced the incidence by 58% as compared with placebo. Metformin therapy reduced the incidence by 31% compared with placebo

LEARNING POINT

Lifestyle changes and metformin therapy reduced the incidence of diabetes in persons at high risk. The lifestyle intervention was more effective than metformin. This study had almost identical findings to the lifestyle intervention in the Finnish Diabetes Prevention study

DREAM

Diabetes reduction assessment with ramipril and rosiglitazone medication

WHO

5,269 individuals with impaired glucose regulation and no previous history of diabetes or cardiovascular disease, randomised using a 2 x 2 factorial design to receive rosiglitazone, ramipril or placebo

WHERE

Multicentre study in Canada

WHEN

Published in 2006

Rosiglitazone: *Lancet* 2006 368: 1096-1105

Ramipril: *NEJM* 2006 355: 1551-2

WHY

To find out whether rosiglitazone or ramipril could prevent the development of type 2 diabetes in people at high risk of developing the condition

WHAT

After a median duration of three years, rosiglitazone reduced the composite primary endpoint of diabetes or death by 60%

There was no significant difference between the groups in the number of deaths or CV events, but the study was not powered to assess these secondary endpoints

The use of ramipril did not significantly reduce the incidence of diabetes or death, but did increase regression to normoglycaemia

LEARNING POINT

Rosiglitazone reduces the incidence of diabetes in high risk individuals. However, other studies have shown that lifestyle interventions, such as increased exercise, weight loss, and dietary changes, can have similar benefits, and should remain the mainstay of prevention of type 2 diabetes (see DPP)

FIELD

Fenofibrate intervention and event lowering in diabetes study

WHO

9,795 patients with type 2 diabetes, aged 50-75 years who were not taking statins at study entry

Undertaken by the FIELD investigators

WHERE

A double-blind, placebo controlled trial in 63 centres in three countries

Published in the *Lancet* 366:1849-61

WHEN

2005

WHY

To examine the effects of long-term fibrate therapy on coronary heart disease event rates in people with diabetes. Patients were randomised to placebo or fenofibrate 200mg daily. Primary endpoint was coronary events, coronary heart disease death and non-fatal MI

WHAT

During the study 17% of the placebo group and 8% of the fenofibrate group started statin therapy

288 patients on placebo and 256 patients on fenofibrate had a coronary event, a non-significant relative risk reduction of 11%. Total cardiovascular events were significantly reduced from 13.9% in placebo arm to 12.5% in fenofibrate arm

A sub-study showed that fenofibrate had no effect on the progression of atherosclerosis (using intimal media thickness)

LEARNING POINT

Fenofibrate therapy did not reduce the risk of the primary outcome. The higher number starting statin therapy in the placebo group may have masked a larger treatment benefit. Fenofibrate did reduce total cardiovascular events

FINNISH (DPS)
The Finnish diabetes prevention study

WHO

Tuomilheto J, Lindstrom J, Eriksson JG et al
522 middle aged, overweight subjects with impaired glucose tolerance, randomised to intensive lifestyle intervention or 'usual care'

Inclusion criteria were: age 40-64, BMI >25kg/m2, and impaired glucose tolerance based on WHO criteria

WHERE

A multicentre study in Helsinki, Turku, Tampere, Kuopio, and Oulu, in Finland

WHEN

2001

WHY

To examine the effect of intensive lifestyle intervention on subjects with impaired glucose tolerance

The control group received general dietary and exercise advice at baseline and had an annual physician's examination. The intervention group received additional individualised dietary counselling from a nutritionist. They were offered physical training sessions and advised to increase overall physical activity. The intervention goals were to reduce body weight, reduce dietary and saturated fat, to increase dietary fibre, and to increase physical activity

WHAT

The study was prematurely terminated by an independent end point committee, as the incidence of diabetes in the intervention group was highly significantly lower than the control group. The risk of diabetes was reduced by 58% in the intensive lifestyle intervention group

LEARNING POINT

Non-pharmacological lifestyle intervention in people at high risk of developing diabetes can prevent or postpone the onset of type 2 diabetes. The observed difference in incidence between the intensive intervention and the usual care group indicates that the intervention needs to be individualised and continuing, and performed by skilled professionals

GREACE

The Greek atorvastatin and coronary heart disease study

WHO

Athyros VG, Papageorgiou AA, Mercouris BR, et al
1,600 consecutive patients, with established coronary heart disease, randomised either to atorvastatin or to 'usual' medical care. The dose of atorvastatin was titrated from 10mg/day to 80mg/day in order to meet the NCEP (National Cholesterol Education Program) target of LDL levels of 2.6 mmol/L

WHERE

Greece!

WHEN

2000

WHY

To assess the effect of atorvastatin on morbidity and mortality (total and coronary) in patients with established coronary heart disease

Primary endpoints of the study were defined as death, non-fatal myocardial infarction, unstable angina, congestive heart failure, revascularisation and stroke

Patients followed for a mean of three years

WHAT

The NCEP treatment goals were met by 95% of patients on atorvastatin. Only 14% of 'usual treatment' patients received any hypolipidaemic drugs during the study

The atorvastatin group had a 49% relative risk reduction in death or recurrent CHD event, as well as lower total mortality and coronary mortality, lower incidence of stroke, and lower coronary morbidity. All subgroups of patients benefited from treatment with atorvastatin

LEARNING POINT

Long-term treatment of CHD patients with atorvastatin to achieve NCEP lipid targets significantly reduced total and coronary mortality, coronary morbidity and stroke, in comparison to patients receiving 'usual' care. Treatment was well tolerated

HOPE

Heart outcomes prevention evaluation trial

WHO

Patients age >55 at high risk of a cardiovascular event because of:

- any evidence of vascular disease

- diabetes plus one other coronary risk factor

9,297 patients randomised to ramipril 10mg per day or placebo, for five years

In addition, all patients were randomly assigned to receive Vitamin E 400 IU/day or placebo

WHERE

Multicentre study

Published in the *Lancet* 355:253-259

WHEN

2000

WHY

A randomised trial of ACE inhibitor, ramipril and Vitamin E in patients at high risk of cardiovascular events, versus placebo

Primary endpoint of the study was the composite of myocardial infarction, stroke or death from cardiovascular causes

WHAT

The safety monitoring board recommended early termination of the study in March 1999, due to overwhelming benefit of ramipril

In the ramipril group, there was a 22% relative risk reduction in the primary outcome measure of death, stroke and MI

All cause mortality decreased by 16%

Ramipril therapy also reduced:

- ◆ onset of new congestive heart failure

- ◆ development of overt nephropathy

- ◆ development of microalbuminuria

The development of diabetes appears to have been reduced by 32% in patients taking ramipril

Overall, the reduction of blood pressure in the ramipril group was 3.3mm Hg, so the benefits on stroke and MI reduction were greater than would be expected by BP reduction alone

Vitamin E had no significant benefits

LEARNING POINT

In a broad range of high-risk patients, ramipril prevents CV death, stroke, heart failure, development of diabetes and diabetes complications, including nephropathy. These benefits are independent of blood pressure lowering.

Vitamin E does not have any significant protective effects

HPS

The heart protection study

WHO

20,536 volunteers in 69 hospitals aged 40-80 years who were at high risk of CHD

It specifically targeted groups of patients in whom there was little direct evidence of benefit from cholesterol-lowering, i.e. women, the over-70s, people with diabetes, those with average or below-average cholesterol levels

WHERE

Undertaken by the Medical Research Council and the British Heart Foundation in the UK

Main results published in the *Lancet* 2002 360: 7-22

Diabetes paper published in the *Lancet* 2003 361: 2005-16

WHEN

Started in 1994, published 2002 and 2003

WHY

To investigate the effects of simvastatin 40mg versus placebo in individuals at high risk of CHD. In a factorial design, half were allocated to receive antioxidant vitamins (600mg Vitamin E, 250mg Vitamin C and 20mg beta-carotene daily)

WHAT

Cholesterol lowering with statin treatment reduced the risk of heart disease and stroke by at least a third, as well as reducing the need for arterial surgery, angioplasty and amputation

These findings apply to:

◆ Women as well as men

◆ People aged over 70 as well as younger people

◆ People with cholesterol levels below 5mmol/L as
well as higher levels

There was no evidence that anti-oxidant vitamins produced any benefits in the groups studied

LEARNING POINT

Individuals with a history of heart attack or stroke, or who are at risk of one, benefit from statin treatment even if their cholesterol levels do not appear to be elevated. The benefits of cholesterol lowering are additional to other treatments, such as aspirin or blood pressure lowering

LIPID

Long-term intervention with pravastatin in ischaemic disease

WHO

9,014 patients aged 31-75 years with a history of myocardial infarction of hospitalisation for unstable angina

Initial plasma total cholesterol levels of 155-271 mg/dl (4-7 mmol/L)

WHERE

Multicentre study

Published in *New England Journal of Medicine* Vol 339:1349-1357

WHEN

Commenced in 1990, published in 1998

WHY

To compare the effects of pravastatin 40mg daily with those of a placebo

Both groups received advice on following a cholesterol-lowering diet

The primary endpoint was mortality from coronary heart disease

WHAT

Mean duration of follow-up was 6.1 years

A relative risk reduction of 24% for death from coronary heart disease in the pravastatin treated group

Overall mortality reduced by 22% in the pravastatin group

Incidence of ALL cardiovascular outcomes was lower in the pravastatin group:

- ◆ myocardial infarction (reduction in risk 29%)

- ◆ death from coronary heart disease

- ◆ nonfatal myocardial infarction

- ◆ stroke

LEARNING POINT

Compared to placebo, pravastatin therapy reduced mortality from coronary artery disease, overall mortality, and other pre-specified cardiovascular events in patients with a history of myocardial infarction or unstable angina, who had a broad range of initial cholesterol levels

MICRO-HOPE
(a subgroup of the HOPE study)

WHO

3,577 diabetic subjects in the HOPE study

WHERE

Multicentre study

Published in the *Lancet* 355: 253-259

WHEN

2000

WHY

A randomised trial of ACE inhibitor ramipril, and Vitamin E in patients at high risk of cardiovascular events, versus placebo

Primary endpoint of the study was the composite of myocardial infarction, stroke, or death from cardiovascular causes

WHAT

Compared to placebo, treatment with ramipril led to:

22% relative risk reduction in MI

33% relative risk reduction in stroke

37% relative risk reduction in cardiovascular death

24% reduction in all cause mortality

LEARNING POINT

In people with diabetes at risk of cardiovascular disease, addition of ramipril reduced cardiovascular death, total mortality, revascularisation, and diabetic nephropathy

MRFIT

The multiple risk factor intervention trial

WHO

316,099 men screened for blood pressure, smoking history and cholesterol status

12,866 men randomised into an 'intervention' group (advised to follow a low-fat diet, stop smoking, hypertension managed according to a pre-set protocol) or 'usual care' (referred to personal physician/GP)

WHERE

Study conducted in the USA

Reported in *JAMA* 248: 1465-77

WHEN

1982

WHY

To evaluate the effect of multiple risk factor intervention on mortality from heart disease in high risk men. Primary end point was death due to coronary heart disease

WHAT

After 6-8 years of follow-up, risk factor levels declined in both groups, but slightly more in the intervention group. Mortality from coronary heart disease and from all causes was not significantly different among the two groups

However, the study showed a continuous association between risk of coronary artery disease and cholesterol level down to 3.0 mmol /L

LEARNING POINT

There was a strong graded relationship between cholesterol levels above 4.65 mmol/L, systolic BP above 110 mm HG, diastolic BP above 70 mm HG and mortality due to CHD. Systolic and diastolic BP, serum cholesterol levels and smoking were significant predictors of death due to CHD in all age groups

The presence of diabetes was equivalent to the presence of two to three risk factors

PROACTIVE

A prospective pioglitazone clinical trial in microvascular events

WHO

Dormandy JA, Charbonnel B, Eckland DJA et al
5,238 patients with type 2 diabetes and evidence of macrovascular disease

WHERE

Multicentre study

Published in the *Lancet* 366: 1279-89

WHEN

2005

WHY

To determine whether pioglitazone reduces macrovascular morbidity and mortality in high risk patients with type 2 diabetes

A prospective, randomised controlled trial, where patients received pioglitazone in doses up to 45mg/day, or placebo

The primary endpoint was the time from randomisation to all-cause mortality, non-fatal myocardial infarction, stroke, acute coronary syndrome, surgical intervention on the coronary or leg arteries, or amputation above the ankle

The main secondary endpoint was a composite of death from any cause, non-fatal MI and stroke

WHAT

Over an average follow-up period of 34.5 months, 19.7% of pioglitazone patients and 21.7% of placebo patients had at least one event in the composite primary endpoint, giving a non-significant reduction of 10% for pioglitazone. The trial thus failed to meet its primary endpoint

The main secondary endpoint occurred in 125 of patients in the pioglitazone group, and 14% of people in the placebo group, giving a statistically significant 16% reduction in relative risk

Over the course of the study, 11% of patients in the pioglitazone group began to use insulin, as compared to 21% in the placebo group, a relative risk reduction of 53%

Heart failure was reported in 11% of pioglitazone patients compared to 8% on placebo, but there was no difference in numbers of deaths from heart failure

Mean weight increased by 3.6kg in the pioglitazone group, compared with 0.4kg decrease in the placebo group

LEARNING POINT

Pioglitazone therapy led to a reduction in the composite of all-cause mortality, non-fatal MI and stroke, in high risk patients with type 2 diabetes. Pioglitazone therapy also reduced the need to add insulin to glucose-lowering regimes

STENO-2

WHO

Gaede P, Vedel P, Larsen N, Jensen GV, Parving HH, Pederson O.
160 patients with diabetes randomly assigned to receive conventional treatment for multiple risk factors from their GP in accordance with national guidelines, or to intensive multifactorial treatment

WHERE

Steno Diabetes Centre, Copenhagen, Denmark

Published in *NEJM* 348: 383-393

WHEN

Initiated in 1992, reported in 2003

WHY

To investigate the impact on microvascular and cardiovascular disorders of a target-driven behaviour modification with polypharmacy, as compared to a conventional multifactorial treatment of high risk type 2 diabetes patients with the metabolic syndrome, including microalbuminuria

The primary endpoint was a composite of cardiovascular disease (non-fatal myocardial infarction, non-fatal stroke, percutaneous coronary intervention and coronary artery bypass grafting) revascularisation of the leg, lower extremity amputation and cardiovascular related death

The goals were HbA1c of 6.5%, blood pressure of 130/80, treatment with ACE inhibitor, treatment with aspirin and a total cholesterol of less than 4.5 mmol/L

WHAT

After 7.8 years, patients in the intensively treated arm had a 53% lower relative risk of cardiovascular disease, and a 20% absolute risk reduction in all-cause mortality

LEARNING POINT

People with type 2 diabetes can significantly reduce their risk of death by intensively treating multiple risk factors

It should be noted that most of the patients did not reach the intensive targets

STOP NIDDM

Study to prevent NIDDM (non-insulin dependent diabetes mellitus)

WHO

Chiasson et al
1,418 people with IGT
(impaired glucose tolerance) – WHO criteria

WHERE

A multinational, multicentre study

Published in the *Lancet*, Vol 359

WHEN

2002

WHY

To study the efficacy of an alpha-glucosidase inhibitor (acarbose) to prevent type 2 diabetes in a population with impaired glucose tolerance

Patients were randomised to placebo or acarbose 100mg tds for four years

WHAT

The risk of developing diabetes was reduced by 25% in the acarbose group. There was also increased reversion of impaired glucose tolerance to normal glucose tolerance

LEARNING POINT

Treatment with acarbose can delay or prevent the progression from impaired glucose tolerance to type 2 diabetes. Flatulence and diarrhoea were common side effects of acarbose therapy

UKPDS

United Kingdom prospective diabetes study

WHO

A large, multicentre randomised clinical trial that followed 5,000+ patients over 20 years

WHERE

23 centres in the UK. Recruitment between 1977 and 1991

WHEN

Results first published in 1998, followed by over 80 subsequent papers

Lancet 1998; 352: 837-53

WHY

To determine whether improved BP and glycaemic control would reduce complications in type 2 diabetes, and to compare therapy with metformin, sulphonylurea, and insulin

WHAT

Intensive treatment with insulin or a sulphonylurea decreased HbA1c in the first year; the levels rose again thereafter, but remained within the target of <7% until year 5

Glycaemic control is not sustained by diet alone or monotherapy with conventional agents in most cases

As type 2 diabetes progresses, glycaemic control deteriorates; this is associated with declining beta-cell function

A 0.9% reduction in HbA1c was associated with a 255 reduction in the risk of microvascular complications

Of the therapies studied, only metformin improved cardiovascular outcomes

Intensive blood pressure control decreases the risk of microvascular and macrovascular complications. Mean achieved BP in the tight control group was 144/82 mmHg, compared with 154/87 in the less tight control group. Tight blood pressure control was associated with a 44% reduction in stroke

LEARNING POINT

This study had a major impact on the management of diabetes. It placed metformin as first line therapy for the majority of patients with type 2 diabetes. It highlighted the progressive nature of the disease, and showed that despite our best efforts, glycaemic control deteriorates with time. The conclusions that have been drawn are that regular monitoring of blood pressure and glycaemic control are essential, and that combination therapy is likely to be needed in the majority of cases.

UKPDS was a huge study, the likes of which we are unlikely to see again. It merits further study, and there are numerous articles, websites and commentaries giving a more detailed perspective

VA-HIT

Veterans administration high density lipoprotein cholesterol intervention trial

WHO

Rubins HB, Robins SJ et al
2,531 men with coronary heart disease and a HDL of 1.04 mmol/L or less and a LDL of 3.63 mmol/L or less

WHERE

USA

Published in *NEJM* 1991: 341 410-418

WHEN

1991

WHY

To investigate the effect of gemfibrozil therapy in patients with existing heart disease and low HDL values

Patients received gemfibrozil 1200mg/day or placebo

WHAT

There was a 24% reduction in death due to CHD, non-fatal MI and stroke in diabetic and non-diabetic patients

There was a 22% reduction in major coronary events in the gemfibrozil group

HDL increased by 6% in the treated group

There was no change in LDL in the treated group

Triglycerides decreased by 31% in the treated group

LEARNING POINT

Death and non-fatal MI was reduced with gemfibrozil. This occurred with a 6% increase in HDL, a 31% decrease in triglycerides, but no change in LDL

WOSCOPS
West of Scotland coronary prevention study

WHO

Shepherd J, Cobbe SM, Ford I et al
6,595 men aged 45-64 with total cholesterol levels of 7.0 + 0.6 mmol/L

No history of coronary disease

WHERE

Multicentre, based in the West of Scotland

Published in *NEJM* 331: 1301-1307

WHEN

1995

WHY

A randomised, double-blind, placebo controlled trial to determine whether pravastatin reduces combined incidence of nonfatal MI and death due to CHD in patients with hypercholesterolaemia. Pravastatin 40mg daily versus placebo

WHAT

Average follow-up was 4.9 years

There was a 31% reduction in non-fatal heart attacks and death from CHD in the pravastatin group

There was a 22% reduction in deaths from any cause in the pravastatin group

There was a 33% reduction in fatal heart attacks in the pravastatin group

LEARNING POINT

Treatment of patients with hypercholesterolaemia, but without existing CHD, using pravastatin, leads to reduction in deaths from fatal MI and non-fatal MI, as well as deaths from any cause

XENDOS

Xenical in the prevention of diabetes in obese
subjects study

WHO

Torgerson JS, Hauptman J, Boldrin M, Sjostrom L
3,305 patients with BMI >30kg/m2, and normal (79%)
or impaired (21%) glucose tolerance, randomised to lifestyle
changes plus either orlistat 120mg or placebo, three times
daily

WHERE

22 Swedish medical centres

Published in *Diabetes Care*: 27, 1, 155-161

WHEN

Study conducted 1997-2002

Published in 2004

WHY

To determine the long-term effect of orlistat in combination
with lifestyle changes in reducing progression to type 2
diabetes in obese, non-diabetic individuals with normal
or impaired glucose tolerance

Primary endpoints were time to onset of type 2 diabetes and
change in body weight. Analyses were by intention to treat

WHAT

Of orlistat treated patients, 52% completed treatment compared with 34% of placebo recipients. After four years' treatment, the cumulative incidence of diabetes was 9.0% with placebo, and 6.2% with orlistat, corresponding to a risk reduction of 37.3%. Mean weight loss was 5.8kg in the orlistat group compared with 3.0kg in the placebo group

LEARNING POINT

Compared with lifestyle changes alone, orlistat plus lifestyle changes resulted in a greater reduction in the incidence of type 2 diabetes over four years and produced greater weight loss in a clinically representative obese population

Glossary

ACEI	angiotensin converting enzyme inhibitor
BMI	body mass index
BMJ	British Medical Journal
BP	blood pressure
CHD	coronary heart disease
CI	confidence interval
CV	cardiovascular
CVD	cardiovascular disease
GI	gastrointestinal
HbA1c	glycosylated haemoglobin
HDL	high density lipoprotein
IGT	impaired glucose tolerance
IU	International Unit
JAMA	Journal of the American Medical Association
LDL	low density lipoprotein
MI	myocardial infarction
NCEP	National Cholesterol Education Program
NEJM	New England Journal of Medicine
NLH	National Library for Health
NNH	numbers needed to harm
NNT	numbers needed to treat
SD	standard deviation
WHO	World Health Organization